Kiss of Christ

Experiencing the Healing
Forgiveness of Jesus
through Confession

Catherine Doherty

Compiled and edited by Jude Fischer

MADONNA HOUSE PUBLICATIONS
COMBERMERE • ONTARIO • CANADA • K0J 1L0

www.madonnahouse.org

Design by Rob Huston

Second printing, December 8th, 2000
Feast of the Immaculate Conception

First printing, January 1st, 1998

Printed in Canada

ISBN 0-921440-64-2

Contents

Foreword

Catherine Doherty, foundress of the Madonna House apostolate, was a woman who loved the Church, and had a deep appreciation of its sacraments. She once said: "The sacraments are Christ's fruit of compassion and mercy, his consolation. With them we can face the heat of the day, we who labor in it. Without them, we can't. The sacraments are an immense love-net of Christ." In this booklet, she gives us some of her reflections on the Sacrament of Penance and Reconciliation.

Selections are included from her talks given between the years 1971 and 1982. It is the custom at Madonna House to have a period of spiritual reading following the noon meal. A passage is read from Scripture or some spiritual book, and this is followed by reflections by community members and guests. During Catherine's lifetime, she usually led these spiritual readings. She read aloud from the selected passage, and then commented. Her talks were informal and spontaneous, flowing from her prayer and Gospel living. They were taped and later transcribed.

Most of the material here is from those talks. Small portions have appeared in some of Catherine's earlier books (*Donkey Bells, Season of Mercy,* and *Welcome Pilgrim*), but most of it is previously unpublished.

This is not intended to be a complete teaching on the sacrament of Penance and Reconciliation. Catherine speaks from the heart of a simple laywoman, leaving to theologians more extensive instruction. She herself urged her listeners to "spend a lot of time in finding out what confession is all about. There are lots of books that deal with confession. Get one and see how important it is." The section in the *Catechism of the Catholic Church* on this sacrament would be a good place to start.

Jude Fischer
Editor

Confession

Today I want to talk to you about Confession. I hope many of you are going regularly. It is one of the most important sacraments of the Catholic Church. Lately people don't go as much as they used to. But confession is such a wonderful thing that everybody should be rushing there. I love confession! Absolution falls on your ears like oil on your wounds. The forgiveness of God envelops you like a mantle. The confessional is the altar of mercy.

At any hour our souls can be washed clean and whiter than snow in the most holy sacrament of Penance. We can become little children again, newly baptized. Think of it, dearly beloved; think of what this most holy sacrament of Confession means. Spendthrift of love, our Lord gives it to us to bathe our souls and make them alive again, resurrecting them from sin in a mercy that knows no end until we die. How utterly loving God is!

If any one of you is away from the sacraments, this is the moment to reconsider. The Father is waiting for you. Why not run to him and say, "I'm sorry."

Instituted by Christ

This beautiful sacrament was instituted by Jesus Christ. He said so clearly to the apostles: "I give you the keys of the kingdom of heaven. Whatever you bind on earth shall be considered bound in heaven. Whatever you loose on earth shall be considered loosed in heaven." And "Receive the Holy Spirit, for those whose sins you forgive, they are forgiven; those whose sins you retain, they are retained" (Matt. 16:19; John 20:22–23).

Now it is a terrible, awesome power that those men have, the successors of the apostles. One of our children, a very ordinary man with humble hands of clay, has a power beyond our understanding, the power to loosen and the power to bind! The mystery of the priesthood is immense. It isn't the priest who is absolving in confession, it's Christ! So why don't we go to confession? It's a marvelous sacrament.

Confession is a psychological need. When I was training in psychiatry, we had a professor who was an atheist, but respected every religion. When he lectured, he used to say to the nurses, "The greatest therapy in the world is the Roman Catholic confession." The Roman Catholic clergy, to their tremendous honor and heroism, have never revealed the secret of the confessional. They have been tortured, they have had terrible things done to them, but they haven't opened their mouth. As a result, there is this man to whom I can go and tell anything and everything, knowing that he is not going to break what they call the seal of the confessional. I can really tell him what is in my heart and the guilt that eats me or whatever. It's rather consoling, isn't it? What is more, the priest says, "I absolve you," and something happens. Suddenly in a very ordinary priest, you feel the immensity of God.

Innocence restored

There is a great miracle in God, a great gift of God—lost innocence can be restored! Have we told others about this gift? Have we spoken to our friends, to our enemies, to ourselves about it—we who are supposedly bringing the Good News to the world? Confession is the way to restore innocence. Once we have repented and have met Christ in this sacrament, he touches us in our inmost being and we become as innocent as new-born babies.

Even though God can restore innocence through this sacrament, we go around very sophisticatedly and say to others: "Oh, you go to confession? You know, that is passé, it just isn't done anymore." I've heard that over and over again! It's another way of taking away from the innocent the return to their innocence. Have we got the right to do this?

Christ's mercy was too immense to allow innocence to be destroyed without showing a way to restore it. So he gave us the sacraments of Penance and of the Eucharist which restore people to pristine innocence. Let us be watchful that we are not guilty of tearing off innocence from anybody. It's a mantle that you can tear off. And if it happens that we do, let us weave a mantle out of our compunction, out of our sorrow, out of our repentance, and put it on that person by leading them to the one place where innocence can be restored, the lips of Our Lord Jesus Christ.

Kiss of Christ

The Russians consider confession "the kiss of Christ." It is Christ's kiss of peace, of forgiveness. When I was a young girl, my mother said, "Catherine, it's time for you to go to confession and be kissed by Christ." Isn't that a nice introduction for a child? So I would go to church, kneel before a priest, and tell him my thoughts.

But in my imagination it was much more than that. My mother very gently and simply explained it. I had committed a fault and knew that God wouldn't like it, so I sort of ran towards him and, sitting on his lap and putting my arms around his neck, I would kiss him—like I did my father—and tell him how sorry I was for having done something he didn't like. In my imagination Christ hugged me and said something like, "That's all right, little girl. I know it's not easy to always do the right thing." Then he would kiss me and bless me and say, "Now go and play."

I realized that when you grow up, you receive another kiss. You sin and say "I'm sorry." Slowly a strange face that nobody knows and yet everybody knows, bends down and touches mine, and I experience the words of the Song of Solomon, "Let him kiss me with the kisses of his mouth" (Song 1:2). Well, this is what confession is. In a sense his lips touch yours, and fire and flame enter your heart and cleanse the sin.

Yes, confession is Christ's kiss of peace, of forgiveness. It's a simple thing, not very complicated. Perhaps the way my mother taught me stayed with me. I was never afraid to go. Always, before my eyes, were the love and forgiveness of God and his immense mercy.

Many people have rejected confession, they are not interested. They don't go there very much. What they miss! They miss being kissed by God. I always feel a little sad when people don't go to confession often, because they miss so much. Above all, they miss a kiss from Christ.

How do you love your enemies? Your neighbor?

The Russian people do not have confessionals. When I was a girl the priest sat under an icon in front of everybody, and you came to him and knelt down and told him your sins. Usually his first question was "How do you love your enemies?"

When I was ten or so I couldn't think of any enemies and he said, "You love all the girls in your class?" I immediately remembered six that I disliked intensely, so he worked on me and changed this. I started loving them, I don't know how.

Then the priest asks you how you love your neighbor, and that is about the end of the conversation, because if you love, you are not going to fornicate, you are not going to commit adultery, you are not going to be avaricious. You are not going to do any of the things that are supposed to be the seven capital sins, because they are all based on charity.

Why don't we all really think today of the second commandment: love your neighbor as yourself. The first neighbor you have, and I have, is ourselves, and I am supposed to love myself in the right way, for I am created in the image and likeness of God. It is strange not to love myself when God loves me. Let us concentrate on what Christ said. Maybe he will help us to love ourselves in such a manner that we are able to love others. For I can't love others until I come to love myself.

Importance of frequent confession

Why is confession so important? If you go to confession often, you sin less. It helps you to overcome any difficulties you may have. Just telling about it makes you think. A tremendous grace is conferred upon a person who confesses often. Strength comes to that person to avoid sin.

We are sinners before God. When we confess our sins, we are washed clean. It is very important to have a clean soul. You can work better. You can do good to other people better when your soul is clean, when your mind is not on yourself. But if you let confession go for two months or so, your soul is in shambles. Everything is topsy-turvy, like pieces of furniture piled on top of one another.

It is so very important to kneel down and say to the Lord, "I am sorry. I am really sorry." To say that in front of another person who is a priest is absolutely necessary. It is all right to say, "I am sorry" to God by yourself, that too is good. But to go to a priest in confession, and acknowledge before someone else that I am in trouble, is very important. You don't know how important it is. If you have forgotten confession, as recently so many have done, remember it again. Go often and you will feel so much better. Your soul will be free of any encumbrances. It makes no difference if it is a small sin or a big sin. The big sins certainly upset you, but the little sins, they pile up, and you have a combination of sins—little sins on top of one another. And at the end you say, "What's the use?" Before you know it you aren't going to church, you aren't going to Communion and so forth. So as a sort of a key to all the other sacraments, confession is of vital importance. I would really spend a lot of time in finding out what confession is all about. There are lots of books that deal with confession. Get one and see how important it is. It is a key to your whole life.

Fear

I was so astonished when I found that people were afraid of confession. Who is afraid of being kissed by Christ? Who can be afraid when he knows he is held tenderly in the hands of Jesus Christ?

I think that the wrong idea of sin is deeply ingrained in so many people.

People are literally afraid when they talk about sin. Sort of a panic gets hold of them. Sin seems to be sort of a mirror that changes them. Like in a carnival midway, you look in one mirror and you are fat, you look in another mirror and you are thin. Well, the idea of sin seems to change a person. They think of themselves as ugly, unpleasant, unlovable, because they say to themselves that they are sinful. Then the spiritual malady, spiritual fear, translates itself into a psychological fear. Which means that we just believe that we're unlovable.

Well, let's look at sin. First, I wish that all Christians thought of themselves as *saved sinners*, because they are. The Lord died on a cross, the Lord resurrected and ascended. What for? To save us. To reconcile us with his Father. Isn't it nice to be a saved sinner?

Sin

What is sin? One of our priests was explaining today at Mass that the word sin means "forgetting" in Hebrew. Its a very good definition of sin. In Russia we don't think of sins as "venial"—or "mortal", either!—we just call them "sins."

Sin means forgetting God. It's a separation from him, a turning of our backs to him. We examine sin usually from the moral aspect. That is a good place to start, because ethics and morality are with us, be we Christians or non-Christians. For Christians it goes deeper. Sin is my rejection of God. I simply say to God, "Look, I am tired of your commandments, and what you eternally ask of me in the name of love. I want to do what I want to do when I want to do it and how I want to do it. And I don't want you to dictate anything to me."

Sin is getting outside of something beautiful, something that is healing, something that is renewing. With God, every

moment is the moment of beginning
again. Yet when we sin, we refuse to
believe that. We reject God, very much as
the Pharisees and a lot of other people he
knew rejected him. Suddenly we find ourselves free to do what we want to do, as
we want to do it, when we want to do it.
Then begins a great tragedy within our
soul, because we find that we are
absolutely tired out. Doing what you
want, as you want, when you want,
doesn't seem to be exactly what you
thought it was. You enter into something
that makes you thoroughly unhappy, and
incidentally makes a lot of psychiatrists
happy. But that's another story.
Psychiatrists have their place, but Christ is
the greatest psychiatrist of all.

Sin is to tear yourself away from the
embrace of God. It's not a question of fear
of hell. It is a question of love, and rejection of love. It might have nothing to do
with an act such as, let's say stealing. It
might have something to do with the inte-
rior you, the unfaithfulness to the Beloved
in a thousand ways that are not visible to

the naked eye. Let us say that I reject one person, one day, just because I am too tired or something. Any sin offends the majesty and goodness of God and breaks the bond of love.

Sin is a terrible thing, an alienation from God, as if I cut with a knife his tenderness, his love. All that he covers me with I reject. I, not he. He will still be there, even if I have rejected everything. You might leave the Church, but the Church hasn't left you! That is the great difference! Christ hasn't left you.

The greatest sin is not to love! All the others flow from that sin, that sin of uncharity. If you want to go to bed with a woman and she isn't your wife, or you want to go to bed with a man and he isn't your husband, that it is a sin against charity! It is a sin of disrespect of one another. If you really love somebody, you don't go to bed with him. You wait until the blessing of God is upon your love. If you steal something, it is against charity. You have deprived someone of their goods, and that is most uncharitable. If you murder someone, that is *very* uncharitable. All sins are against charity.

All sins, no matter how small or how big, mortal or venial, break love in some way. It breaks my love toward God. And that is tragic. The saddest thing in the world is to be alienated from God. Let us run into God's arms and make up!

It is so simple. It is just one confession. "Father, I have sinned against charity," and that is all there is to it, fundamentally! Oh, it's all right to define things and so forth, but fundamentally we only need to say, "Father, I have sinned against love." It is like a dirge in your soul that rises and sings its lament, "Father, I have sinned against love." Suddenly Christ bends and kisses you. The kiss of Christ is the pain of Christ, but the kiss is also the freedom of Christ. So when I open my heart in confession and say, "Lord, I have sinned against love, have mercy on me," down comes this mercy, and you return to being a child of God. Now you are among the children who are around him, about whom he says to the apostles, "Let the little children come to me, and do not stop them. Unless you are like these children, you are not going to enter the kingdom of heaven" (see Luke 18:15–17).

Christ came to restore sinners. He became the one who took all our sins upon his shoulders. So we are the beloved, his beloved, the ones he rescued from sin. But man, being what he is, or she is, falls along the narrow road, for temptations, like boulders, are strewn on the path. And so, we come back to Christ again. This time, we say to him, "Lord, kiss our sins away." For that is what confession is, the kiss of Christ.

Free will

The greatest thing that we have is free will. We can sin, and we can not sin. We can do good, and we can do evil, and that makes the difference between us and all the rest of creation.

"If you wish you can keep the commandments. They are within your power" (Sir. 15:15). The amazing part is that God, in his infinite mercy, took the power that he had, for God is all-power, and simply restrained it, in regard to man. He gave man the commandment of love, and he left him free to practice or not to practice it. It is up to you! You don't have to! Nobody puts a pistol to your head. You can do whatever you like, and that is the miracle of God's goodness, of God's mercy, and the strange, incomprehensible respect that he has towards man. The psalmist says, "What is man that you should pay attention to him?" (Ps. 8). He is just a speck on the horizon before the Lord. Yet what more can you ask of God than to withhold his power? He could annihilate us in a second. He could make us slaves in a minute if he wanted to, so that we would act like little puppets, but he didn't do any of those things. He left us free! This is the most beautiful thing in the world—to be free before God! To choose between good and evil. God has created you in his image. He has allowed you to choose and to know that he is also there to help.

Loss of sense of sin

We can never condone sin, but we must always love the sinner. It is as simple as that. But in the sixties, through the hippies, the intellectuals, the liberals and others, we began to excuse sin. The sense of sin has almost disappeared these days. People sin and don't know that they're sinning. Sin is called anything but sin. There is an interesting book called *Whatever Became of Sin*, by Dr. Karl Menninger, an outstanding psychiatrist. He found that people who had been supposedly "liberated" by psychiatrists became worse off later on. There was no healing through eliminating the notion of sin. Now, coming from a world-renowned psychiatrist like Dr. Menninger, this is really something.

The average Russian would never deny that sin is a sin. He will never excuse a sin. He will say that adultery is adultery, and I have committed adultery. Fornication is fornication, and I have committed fornication. Lying is lying, and I have lied. Stealing is stealing, and I have stolen.

I remember the sixties and the hippies, who were going around saying that there was no God, and you fell in everybody's bed and you did anything you wanted. If you mentioned the word *sin*, they laughed. But strangely enough, if you were listening with your heart—not only with your ears—you heard them cry. You just can't push things around like that, because sin exists, it's a reality.

You have to love the sinner and hate the sin, and put squarely before people what sin is and never condone it. But love, cherish and heal the sinner, for God came for sinners. In the sixties, the lines got blurred. We have to watch out for that if we are to be instruments of God's healing.

There was a girl who came to me and said that she had slept with forty-eight men. Well, that was in the hippy days, and she was egged on by her Catholic friends, for it was a Catholic college. It was one of those crazy experiments. When we talked about it, I was struck by two aspects of the situation. First, she was very innocent when she left home for college. Secondly, she was exceedingly frightened of sex. Mama was a Jansenist and warned her much too much. Also, she was pushed into this by her peers. We discussed all this: what was her sin, what was not her sin, what was the sin of Mama, what was the sin of the kids who pushed her. Finally I said "How do you feel?" She said, "Like a second-hand piece of goods, sold in some lousy basement on some tenement street." She knew perfectly well that ultimately she was not guilty before her mother, nor before her peers. That's when she fell on her knees, put her head in my lap, and started crying, because she knew she was guilty before God. That was the moment when I said, "Go to confession to receive the kiss of Christ. That will erase all those evil kisses you have received through the years. For God is merciful."

Our sin affects the whole world

Sin makes God sad, and his Church sad too, since you are his Church. We are the People of God. When I commit a sin, you all suffer. If you commit a sin, we all suffer. Because of that, I think all sins are tragic.

The East is not worried about its sins, juridically speaking. The East weeps over its sins because they are an offense against charity, against love for God and one's fellowmen. For when I commit a sin, even if it's alone in my apartment or hidden in the dark recesses of my soul, I sin against the whole Body of Christ, against all the People of God. No matter how hidden my sin, it reverberates across the rest of the world. For I'm so deeply united with all the rest of mankind that what I do and what I don't do affects the whole world.

Faith is a mystery, a gift of God which joins us in the brotherhood of Christ—for Christ died for the Buddhists, the atheists, the Moslems, the Christians and everybody. He's the brother of man. Anything that goes against love is sin. St. Augustine said, "Love and do what you will," because if you love, you won't hurt anybody. It is in Christ that the brotherhood of man is established. That men understand God in various stages, differently, is neither here nor there. Ultimately, all things come together in the apex of Christ, the whole cosmos comes together. And so, what I do affects everybody.

I'm a nurse and am taking care of a patient. I get a little pinprick from his splinter. It's very small, but the next day I feel pain. If I don't take care of it, I may develop an infection from some germ that will spread, and I may die. Sin is like that pinprick. It affects the body, the Mystical Body of Christ.

Examination of conscience

What does it mean to examine one's conscience? It means to recollect oneself, to collect all the fragments. We have to become still and not allow our heart or mind to be buzzing like flies. In total stillness, with a firm resolve, we begin to descend into our heart and there we find that which has to be thrown out. That is an examination of conscience. Most of the things that have to be thrown out will deal with selfishness.

How much do I love? How often in my life does the pronoun *I* disappear, replaced by the words *they, we, he*, or *she*? In this we have a very simple yardstick of love. Let's say a thought comes into your mind, "I want to do this." If it is something God would like you to do, go ahead and do it. If not, erase it, and keep on erasing it! The word *I* will disappear and someday perhaps we will kneel and kiss the feet of somebody else. The sins against charity, the sins of pride, the sins of indifference to others, to my brothers and sisters—those are the sins that bite!

So many of us are Judases, betraying Christ with a kiss, so to speak. How do you feel—how do I feel—when in some sort of a way we betray Jesus Christ? It's a very subtle thing. I think that's one of the grave sins. People are worried about sex sins. Sex has been created by God, but pride, arrogance, and all those kind of things, have not been created by God. Our betrayals are so subtle. I think we should examine our conscience very deeply, because this sort of thing escapes us so very quickly. We have an ability to rationalize whenever we discuss the Gospel. We water down, rationalize, find excuses for not doing what we know we should.

Our confessions can be superficial and not go deep enough. If they are superficial, we haven't really gone into the caverns and caves of our souls. We've wrapped a lot of things in cellophane and stuck them on the shelves of the caverns, when they should have been brought forth. But we let them be, and like splinters they fester in our soul. We are not in truth, and we have left integrity behind somewhere.

Christ is a revolutionary. He calls us to give the whole of ourselves. He calls us to perfection. In Russia we have no distinction between a Trappist and a father of a family, between a married woman and a Trappistine. We believe that Christ said "Be ye perfect..." (Matt. 5:48) to everybody, because we believe that in Baptism the little feet begin the journey of union with God.

Let us look into our own hearts. Let us see the mess that is there. Why can't we bring it all out? Why don't we make a clean sweep of it? Where has my heart wandered? To what places has it gone? How far away from God am I? Why?

You see yourself, but you never despair, because along with your sins you see the mercy of God. You look at yourself. You realize the depth and the breadth of sin. Then you look at God and say, "Lord, have mercy on me." In the process you forget yourself. You begin to contemplate God, and all else disappears in him.

We make believe that we're Catholics. We talk about the Scriptures. But the Scriptures are empty words unless you put them into practice. It's useless to listen with one ear, and let it out of the other ear, and do nothing about it. It will be held against you if you know the Scriptures and don't apply them. The Gospel is so limpidly clear. It's addressed to ordinary people, just like you and I. Look deep down into your soul. Look into it, see what's wrong, throw it out, bring Christ in! There is so little time.

Guilt

We are riddled with guilt. One of the things everyone is worried about is God's justice. People shake and say, "Oh, I am a louse, I am a sinner." Of course you are a sinner! But never forget you are a *saved* sinner. Why is everyone going around wallowing in their past sins? We go to confession and we say, "Oh, I don't feel that I am cleansed." When you really repent, you are as clean as a little newborn baby! What's the score? Why should I worry about what happened to me or the last mortal sin that I committed? God has forgotten it, so why should I remember?

When we continue to feel guilty, there is something behind it—there is lack of trust in God. Oh yes, we know that God forgives sinners! We believe it. But do we? So we say! But where is our confidence in God, our love of God, our trust in God, our faith, and our hope? Where are they? If they were there we would not be racked with guilt.

The Russians very seldom feel guilty, because, you see, they rely on the mercy of God very strongly, and they go to confession. The only time that I feel guilty is the time between the committing of the sin and going to confession. But when I'm absolved I forget that I ever sinned. Why should I remember if God doesn't? Think about it.

God is merciful to repentant sinners. Yet in our society there is this terrible emotional problem of guilt. You can tell people again and again that God forgives, but they refuse to believe it. In the first place they refuse to believe that he loves them; and they refuse to believe that he loves them because they don't forgive themselves. They say, "If I cannot forgive myself, how can God?" Again, our little peanut brains want to reduce God to our own stature. It is a tragic situation, because if only we accepted this premise that God forgives us, we would be a laughing, joyous, guiltless, happy generation.

Consider the ways of God with men. To begin with, the most strange thing really is true: God loved us first. Now, try to absorb this—absorb it! Take it into your skin, into your pores, into everything. God loved us first! Well, we are not very lovable, but somehow or other he managed it. He loved us first. The picture of Christ is one of such gentleness. He looks at us, and he loves us so much. He wants to take us and press us to his Heart. But we say "No, no!" We don't want to hear this stuff. Still he loves us. He continues to love us to the very end.

Why don't we approach God with the utter simplicity of children? Suppose we lived in Nazareth when he lived there. He would have attracted us by his personality. I am sure lots of young people and old people talked to him. He was wise. And they were peaceful about it and happy. But we are forever searching our hearts with our little peanut brains, that's our problem!

God's way with man is so gentle, so gentle. He was accused of hobnobbing with prostitutes and tax collectors, and he did. When he was speaking, to whom was he talking? Mostly to cooks and waiters— ordinary people. The "big shots" were at the back, writing down something on their tablets to condemn him with. Very few of them came to him, only the poor, the humble, the unimportant. They came, that's the kind of people he liked. And that's the kind of people we all are. God deals with all of us with great gentleness, and always with great kindness. It's *we* who attribute to him great severity, the big stick and so forth.

Why do we go around thinking that we are the lousiest people on earth, with a self-image almost of despair? Why attribute that sort of lousy self-image to oneself, when (a) I have been created by God; (b) I am an icon of God; (c) He died to save me. I am loveable, and so I cannot have a lousy image of myself unless I have a lousy image of God.

To us are addressed the words in Isaiah: "I am he who blots out your transgressions," said the Lord. "No need to recall the past. No need to think about what was done before" (Isa. 43:25, 18). On reading that, can anyone have a feeling of guilt left?

How can a Christian feel guilty once he has read the Gospel? A thief asked Jesus, "Remember me when you come into your kingdom." Jesus replied, "Indeed, I promise you, today you will be with me in paradise" (Luke 23:35–43). This word of a man on a cross, dying for love of humanity, is a consolation for all who feel guilty because of sins. Let guilt be wiped out. "Today you will be with me in paradise." If any one of you feels guilty and you know that you deserve it, fear not. Look at Jesus Christ. If you say, "Have mercy on me" and look with eyes of faith, you will see an unseen hand wipe out all your sins and misdemeanors. You will realize that you are already in paradise, because he who is merciful dwells in you, and where he is, there is paradise. It is as simple as that.

Who can feel guilty when he is held by the hand of mercy? If I repent, I simply say, "Sorry, Lord," and he has already forgiven. Place yourself before Jesus Christ, and slowly fear will leave, and guilt will leave, and we will be left a sinner who has started to love. Look at the Prodigal! Think about it. Cheer up! There is nothing to worry about.

Guilt vs. sadness

It is incredible that a Christian should continue to feel guilty after confession. I can understand that he feels exceedingly sad. I can understand when he feels like crying. The Russians always pray for the gift of tears, because we say that the tears wash guilt away, among other things. How can I remain guilty when I am pardoned the moment I say I am sorry? That I can feel the alienation between myself and Christ, sure! When I remove myself from Christ because I have sinned, then all the sadness of the world can come into my heart, but guilt cannot linger there. How can I forget that God is merciful? This is the strangest difference between the East and the West. I explained to God that I would like to have five minutes of guilt as the Canadians and Americans feel it, so that I could come to them and say, "Oh yes, now I know how you feel." But I don't know how to be guilty. I know how to weep. I know how to be sad. I know how to cry in the night. But I don't know how to be guilty! Because there is a Gospel! And every guilt is covered by the mercy of God.

Across the centuries a voice says, "Judge not and you will not be judged" (Matt. 7:1). How can one read the Gospel and doubt the mercy of God?

So you who cry in the night and who weep in the day, be at peace. Be at peace. Whatever guilt there has been, he has risen and his blood has washed it away.

You can come to him and make a cup out of your hands, and one drop of this blood, symbolically, will clean you if you have faith in his mercy. And if you say four little words: "Lord, I am sorry."

Of course, if you have mortal sin on your soul, go to a priest, because Christ gave them the key. When we confess a grave sin, hope like a light, like a song, should surge in us, not guilt that leads to despondency, anger, despair and what have you, but hope!

A Christian can have sorrow, a gentle sorrow, and a new prayer for faith that one may not commit what one has done before. But lingering guilt should be totally alien to him if he has faith, for if he has faith he knows the mercy of God. Let us lay guilt aside. But let us pray for the gift of tears. Let us pray for the gift of love so as not to sin. Let us pray for simplicity, the simplicity of a child who has just broken Mama's favorite cup and runs into her arms and says, "I am sorry." When you are not filled with guilt you can begin to think about the mercy of God and lots of other things that you can pass on to others to the best of your ability.

Don't hold on to your guilt. Set your doubts aside. Put all that in a sort of bundle and throw it out. Here is faith, that belief stronger than death. It is as if hail was falling on the roof and we are all warm inside. So there is hail on the roof, but in your heart there is a flame, and in your soul there is love that is stronger than death. You believe and nothing that may happen to you or to me in this world makes any difference. He is in our midst. The advocate, the helper of the poor, is by my side! What have I to fear? Nothing!

Genesis

Did you ever read Genesis? God the Father is angry, throwing Adam and Eve out of paradise. But have you ever noticed that while he was doing this he was making them nice warm coats, because outside of paradise it is cold (Gen. 3:21)! So his anger was tempered with his mercy even then. Then he gave them a big speech. He told them about a woman that was going to crush the serpent who had crushed them (Gen. 3:15). He told them many things that were kind of cheerful, and we sing at Easter, "O happy fault." We are almost grateful, in fact we are grateful, that Adam and Eve got thrown out of paradise, because that brought us Christ! Reread Genesis and think!

David

David acknowledged his sins. That was his greatest claim to fame. He fell in love with a woman who had a husband who was an army officer. He sent him far away to be killed, and he lived with the woman; but he repented, loudly and brilliantly. In one of the psalms it is mentioned how he repented. That kind of person should be close to us. (See 2 Sam. 11:2–12:15; Ps. 51).

Prodigal son

Recently I reread the story of the Prodigal Son (see Luke 15:11–32). I often read it. It is one of my favorite parables. And I said to myself, now think about it, Catherine. Think about it with your heart, not with your head. It is the heart that understands. The head understands a little, but the heart understands much more.

There was a father, and he had two sons. One son wanted his inheritance immediately. He wanted everything *now!* Not tomorrow, not yesterday—now. Now the father, being a father, knows very well what is going to happen to the one who claims his inheritance. He has been around long enough. But he gives it to him. And so it happens that the son turns to wine, women and song—riotous living. Finally he is reduced to looking after swine. Nobody seems to give him much to eat, so he eats the husks and food given to the swine. Then he has a brilliant idea. He thinks, it would be so much better to go and be a servant in my father's house, because at least they will feed me. And so he goes.

What happens to the father? I read in between the lines sometimes. I have a vivid imagination, so don't think that what I saw is exactly how it is said in the Gospel. But reading it over and over again, I can just see the father, periodically going outside and looking, straining his eyes, just hoping that there beyond the horizon, his son will come. One day as he was looking, lo and behold, there in the distance he saw a speck. But he knew who it was, he recognized him, as only fathers and mothers can do. He immediately called a servant. First he ran towards the approaching silhouette. But as he ran he must have asked the servant to bring a ring and lovely cloak. And the father and son meet! The son fell on his knees and begged pardon of his father. But before the words were out of his mouth, the father picked him up and pressed him to his heart, and in a spirit of tremendous joy put the ring on his finger and covered his rags with this beautiful cloak.

This is what God does to us, over and over and over again! The Lord, like the father, puts a ring upon my finger. It is a seal upon my heart of his forgiveness.

Christ and sinners

Then there is the story of the woman caught in adultery. The Jews found this woman in adultery, and they brought her before Christ. What does Christ do? He wasn't even curious. He evidently turned his back and was writing something in the sand. Then quietly, from the back, he said. "Whoever of you is without sin, throw the first stone," and he went on writing.

Look at the delicacy. He turned his back to that woman. She was ashamed to be before this prophet, and so delicately he turned his back, because he was a lover of men. So after awhile he said, "Woman, did anybody condemn you, throw the stones?" There was no one to throw stones, because the Jews had sense enough to disappear; there wasn't one of them without a sin. So Christ said to her very peacefully, "Go in peace, and sin no more" (John 8:3–11).

Once he was invited to some kind of dinner, where there was a woman of ill repute—a beautiful woman—who was washing his feet with her tears and drying them with her beautiful hair. Throughout the room there was the scent of this fragrant ointment that she was pouring on his feet. The people who had invited him—the big shots, the VIPs—were thinking and whispering among themselves, "If he is really a prophet, he would know who this woman is who is touching him." Jesus turned around and said, "Look, you didn't give me a kiss. You didn't pour oil on my head." All the politeness and kindness that Jews extend to Jews when they invite each other to dinner, this man hadn't done for Christ. "But she is doing this." Then he turned around and told her that she loved much and her sins were forgiven (see Luke 7:36–50).

What must Peter have felt when Christ appeared to him after his resurrection and said, "Peter, do you love me?" three times (John 21:15–17). He must have felt liberated from the terrible sin of betrayal. Christ never spoke of his betrayal. Peter went around talking about it everywhere, but Christ never mentioned it.

Christ said, "There will be more rejoicing in heaven over one repentant sinner than over ninety-nine virtuous men who have no need of repentance" (Luke 15:7). There are the parables of the lost drachma and the lost sheep (Luke 15:4–10). All these parables say the same thing. The message is clear—extra love is poured out on the repentant sinner, and the greater the sinner, the greater God's

love, and the greater the joy in heaven.
Doesn't that bring hope? Doesn't it make
you throw your guilt out?

St. Paul

*I thank Christ Jesus our Lord who has given
me strength and who judged me faithful
enough to call me into his service, even
though I used to be a blasphemer and did all
I could to injure and discredit the faith.
Mercy, however, was shown me, because
until I became a believer I had been acting in
ignorance and the grace of our Lord filled
me with faith and with the love that is in
Jesus Christ. Here is a saying that you can
rely on and nobody should doubt: that
Christ Jesus came into this world to save
sinners. I myself am the greatest of them.
And if mercy has been shown to me, it is
because Jesus Christ meant to make me the
greatest evidence of his inexhaustible
patience for all the other people who would*

later have to trust in him to come to eternal life. (1 Tim. 1:12–16)

Paul was a big sinner. He tried to destroy the Christians. Suddenly the inexhaustible mercy and forgiveness of God touched him and he fell off his horse. He was blind for a little while, but he received the gift of faith and he passed it on (see Acts 9:1–19; 22:5–16; 26:9–18). But he acknowledges himself to be a sinner! That is beautiful!

He had no guilt complex! He was absolutely sure he was going to get this crown of righteousness, because he knew the merciful God. If anybody knew about mercy, it was Paul! He was persecuting all the Christians; he was killing people. Then God zapped him. Paul had been full of hatred himself. Later when he was testifying for God, everybody deserted him. What does he say? Immediately he says: may they not be held guilty. Remember that. It is a very good point for all of us to remember. Sometimes God offers us very difficult choices, and this is one. But thanks be to God, Paul flew through it like an angel. He forgave everybody (see 2 Tim. 4: 6–8, 16–18).

We are all sinners

Baptism washes away our sin. But we're still human. We can sin anytime. God loves sinners. He knows we're sinful. He knows that after Baptism we will continue to sin, that we will be falling down flat on our face all the time. So he has given us the sacrament of Penance.

We are all sinners. Out of the depths I cry to thee, O Lord. Behold my day. I haven't swept, I haven't dusted, I haven't tended to my children, I have double-crossed my husband, I have been taken in adultery. Behold me! And a man is writing on the sand, "Woman, has anybody condemned thee?" "No, sir." "Neither do I. Go and sin no more" (John 8:8–11).

Yes, we are all sinners. But let us never forget that we are *saved* sinners. That we are going to fall down a thousand times between birth and death is rather obvious. But immediately we look at the Gospel and see that God came for sinners, not for the perfect ones, if there be such. No. He said, "I did not come to call the just but the sinners" (Matt. 9:13). That means every one of us. Three cheers! You don't have to be perfect to be loved by God.

Yesterday somebody was talking to me and she said, "But I lack virtue. I am not up to par in fidelity. I am not good in this and in that." She really felt deeply that she wasn't worthy of God because she wasn't full of all those virtues. But that is not what God wants! I said, "Have you ever considered that God loves sinners? And that we are all saved sinners?" She said, "Yes, I know we are sinners, that is what bothers me." I said, "That is what should cheer you up!"

Christ came into the world to save sinners. The majority of people say yes to this with their lips but not with their heart. They do not believe completely, totally and without a single doubt that Christ came to this world to save sinners. They think that they should work hard so that God approves of them. They are going to get to heaven on their own efforts! Instead of remembering that Christ said, "Without me you can do nothing" (John 15:5). The result is a very great tragedy.

You don't need to wallow in guilt. Wallow in the mercy of God. When you are guilty, say so to God through a confessor. Acknowledge your problems and sins. The moment you have stated them, God puts his hand over you and you are a newborn babe. With God every moment is the moment of beginning again. So cheer up, folks! Especially you young ones who are eternally worrying about the unnecessary things. Sure, we are sinners. We will fall down. But the arms of God are immense, and they embrace everybody.

Judgment of God

Some people are afraid of the judgment of God. God sent his Son and we say "God is love." Now how does Love judge? Take the example in the Gospel of a woman taken in adultery. First, delicacy. Turning around and not looking, and writing something in the sand. Then saying, "Go and sin no more" (John 8:11). You can feel the gentleness and goodness of that voice.

Next to Christ on the cross is a thief. Christ says to him, "Today you shall be with me in paradise" (Luke 23:43). That's the judgment of Christ!

Then there was Mary Magdalene who was one of the women who followed him and who was not exactly what she should be. One doesn't hear that in that Gospel, except that whoever invited him for dinner was astonished that he allowed a prostitute, a woman with a bad name, to wash his feet and dry them with her hair. And then he turned around and said,

"Much is forgiven her because she loves much" (Luke 7:47).

To me the judgment of Christ is mercy and tenderness and gentleness, and I have never had any fear of judgment, provided I say I am sorry! I would tremble in my boots if I didn't say "I am sorry." That's a different story!

Mercy of God

The mercy of God is beyond our understanding. It is given to us no matter who we are and what we are. Now do we or don't we believe in his mercy? Do we face a very simple thing? That what comes out of the hands of God cannot be ugly, deformed, lousy. Now how can you have a wrong image of yourself when you know that you come from the hands of the loving God? Look at your face in a mirror, and you see God's image. "Whatsoever you do to the least of my brethren you do to me" (Matt. 25:40). Why do we pull our-selves down? Why are we worried? Why are we trying to get people to approve of us? Have we forgotten that we were cre-ated and loved by God himself? Have we forgotten the Incarnation? The Crucifixion? The Resurrection? The Ascension? Have we forgotten the mercy of God?

Do you feel the warmth of God's mercy? Do you feel the tenderness that embraces you? Do you hear that knock at your heart that says "You don't need to be lonely and worried about this. I am with you, I am in you. I am among you." Do you feel his consolation? And I mean feel not in any psychological sense, but in a spiritual sense in faith. Do you feel the touch of his hand upon your heart, healing the wound you have made through sin?

We are human. Unfortunately, we are likely to sin in one way or another. It will take us a long time to get over it. But in the moment we have sinned—that very moment—we should cry out to God,

"Lord, have mercy," and then go to confession about it.

Don't let sin twist you. Don't let him who induces you into sin make you feel that, because you sinned, you're cut off from God. Tell Satan, "Go where you belong, and stay there." Confess, "I have sinned; I'm sorry; Lord, have mercy on me." And listen to the devil sizzle as he goes down. Just listen to him sizzle. The moment you say, "Lord, have mercy," Satan disappears.

You may say that this is an almost infantile approach to sin. But I don't think so. I think that it's an approach in faith, the great and deep faith that God alone can give us, and for which we must pray. For faith alone can cure this wrong image of sin, this fear. It comes down to faith. Faith believes unshakably in the mercy of God, and realizes that unless I am merciful, I shall not find mercy. If I believe God is merciful, then out of the very depths of my soul, comes my mercy, which is his, given to everyone. Have you ever experienced the mercy of someone? If you ever have experienced it, you know its tender-ness and warmth.

So if anyone of us sins again, let us be peaceful about it, sorrowful, sad, but also filled with gratitude that we are able to say, "Lord, have mercy." Then we receive his mercy.

That doesn't mean that we should go around saying, "Well, because he's merci-ful, I'm going to sin." No! On the con-trary, "Because he's merciful, I shall be merciful." But if we have fallen, his hand reaches out, he takes us close to his bosom, and presses us to his heart. God is so simple! We have problems, but God is simple. Go to him like a child.

Repentance

Here we enter into a strange word that in the East means so much more. What does repentance mean to the West? It means many things. It means sorrow, sad-

ness, a cry for forgiveness, officially enter-
ing into a confessional. All these things are
there in the Russian church too. But to the
Russian people, repentance is a "bright
sadness." When a Russian begins to feel
the grace of repentance, which is a gift
from the Holy Spirit, he thanks God for
the ability to be repentant—even though
he isn't moving anywhere yet. Then he
begins to cry. It comes spontaneously. He
hasn't yet gone to confession. He's not
even thinking about going to confession.
He is in his sadness.

To the Russian, sin is sadness. It carries little guilt, but it carries a lot of sadness. So he cries. Then after he has seen
what he has done to God, he sits down
and begins to look at God and says, "Oh, I
have crucified God. I mean, my sins were
part of his death. But look—beyond
Golgotha, there is Easter!" And in the
Russian heart, hope springs up.

I'm not a theologian, I'm just telling
you how I and many of my countrymen
feel. Repentance shot through with hope
is a most fantastic and beautiful thing. You

can almost dance. So, he who cried, dances towards the church to go to confession, because he has seen the bright side of sadness. Now, with great joy, he goes to confession, because in his mind something has happened. He feels himself a child. Do you wonder that I say: "Lord, give me the heart of a child, and the awesome courage to live it out?" At that moment of bright sadness, or repentance, he feels himself a child. But so totally that he says to himself: "Ha, let me *run* to God! The lap of the Father is waiting, I'll jump into it, put my arms around his neck, and I'll say to him, 'Father, I have sinned, but I love you.' What is God going to do, it's obvious! He is going to kiss me back." All this is connected by him with the Resurrection. We love confessions; we're not afraid of them.

To me, repentance is 'making new.' With God, every moment is the moment of beginning again. Every time I repent over my sins, over my mistakes, over all these things, I renew myself in the sacrament of Penance, and from the sacrament of Penance I come as a newborn child out of the water of Baptism. I am renewed and full of grace, and this is why I hope you will never feel guilty, because the guilt has been washed out with every repentance. That is the amazing thing about God.

Jesus began his preaching with this message: "Repent, for the kingdom of heaven is close at hand" (Matt. 4:17). The key to the entry into the kingdom of heaven which is within us is repentance. We see it throughout the whole Gospel, and it is so beautiful. People asked him to heal them and he said, "Arise, your sins are forgiven you." "Your faith has made you whole." Over and over again. Faith and repentance have made you whole. When I sometimes attend prayer meetings and people ask for healing, I ask for their repentance in my heart, because the healing will not take place until repentance takes place. I don't know if they have anything to repent for, but I think all of us have, so why not pray for repentance? They would rather pray for healing—

same thing! Without one there is not the other!

Repentance is not a confession of past sins only. Repentance is a turning around. Some people think that if I sin, then I apologize and go to confession and get forgiven and all the rest of it, I have repented. No! Repentance is much more than that. Repentance is really doing that which I know I must do. Repentance is the incarnation of the Gospel in a person's life.

Yes, I have acknowledged that I have sinned before the Lord. I have acknowledged that I have trodden the wrong path. This I have done. But now I must turn my back to all of that and move in the opposite direction. Otherwise, in a little while, I will be telling the same story all over again to another priest or to the same priest.

To repent is to change. It is not just to acknowledge that I have done wrong. It is to turn my back to the wrong and start doing right, incarnating the Gospel. On this hinges the answer of Christianity to the world of today. The world of today doesn't believe that what Christ taught us is of any value, because we do not incarnate it.

How are we going to do it? In a sense it is awfully simple. We just have to stop personality clashes, judgment of one another, mistrust of one another, anger against one another, hostility against one another. We have to begin to love one another as Christ loved us. Then the pagans of today will say, "Look at those Christians! They've really got something. See how they love one another!"

Yes, repentance is more than penitence. It is not remorse. It is not admitting mistakes. It is not saying in condemnation, "I've been a fool." Who of us has not recited such a dismal litany? All of us have. They are common and easy to recite. Repentance is more. It is even more than being sorry for one's sins. It is a moral and spiritual revolution. To repent is one of the hardest things in the world, yet it is basic to all spiritual progress. It calls for a complete breakdown of pride, of self-assurance, of prestige that comes from success, of the innermost citadel of self-will.

God comes to us, tenderness, forgiveness, love, calling us to repentance, so that he might embrace us; so that he might bring us peace. What are we going to do? Unless we turn to him, we shall perish.

Bringing our repentance to God

How is repentance brought to God? Obviously, if you live on an island all by yourself, or if you are somewhere far away where priests can not come, or if you are alone when you are dying, you don't have to go to any priest to confess. There are thousands of reasons why you cannot reach a priest.

But normally speaking, for Catholics, the channel to grace is confession. Repentance comes, the cry comes out of our heart, and we go to confession. We go to the man God has appointed, and share our sins. If you live in Timbuktu where there is no priest, or somewhere where a priest comes once a year, well, talk to God and he will absolve you; and when the priest comes, talk to him about it. It's so simple!

The person who listens to your confession has one job: first, to love and to give the kiss of Christ and his mercy and forgiveness and so forth; and secondly, to lead you to God in ever mounting steps. He becomes, as it were, the Jesus Christ who says "Come higher, friend." But in this case, of course he is not God, and he says, "Take my hand and let's go higher toward Jesus Christ."

Let us put it in simple language. My mother had a very precious cup that she had left on the table, and she said to me, "Catherine, don't touch this cup. Don't break it; it's a precious cup." Now at the age of five or so that begins to be interesting! So I circled around the table for awhile, then finally I picked it up, and eventually it broke. So I thought it over and put it into a wastebasket, considering that what you don't see, you might forget! When mother came back and looked, there was no cup on the table, and she asked, "Catherine, did you touch the cup?" At this point I felt that it wasn't right to have done all those things, and something in me said I had better confess and tell her how sorry I was. So I did, and my mother put me on her lap and said, "I'm glad you have been truthful and are sorry. You are a good little girl. Let's kiss one another. I forgive you; it's okay. But you broke the cup, didn't you?" I said, "Yes." She said, "Well, you have to pay a little for it. So you will give me two cents a week from your allowance so that you know there are certain things you have to repair." Now wasn't that just? And it reminded me not to break other cups!

So sacramental Confession is you coming to God and saying, "I am really sorry about that broken cup. Here I am, I confess it and I am in full repentance about it." And God embraces you again! My going and apologizing to the cook about my mother's cup wouldn't get me anyplace in my mother's heart. I had to talk to my mother, to the person to whom this cup belonged. Well, the same with confession. This is why personal confession, "eyeball to eyeball," instead of only general confession, is important. The Church sometimes allows general confession. For instance, during the war when there was no time to form a line before a single chaplain, the Church gave absolution to thousands of people, who, of course, had in their heart a great sorrow and repentance. But though it is permitted now in certain circumstances, I think it's kind of nice to talk to Jesus Christ about things that you want to hide from other people and then get absolved. That voice that is talking through Father A or Father B, or whoever, is Christ's voice, and it is kind of nice to hear Christ's voice, provided you believe what a priest is.

To me, in my deep faith, any priest is Christ when he is exercising his powers. I kneel before him, but it is not him; in my mind it is Christ. When I kneel and tell him

"Forgive me, Lord," quietly, deeply, Christ kisses my forehead and says, "I absolve you," and now I am absolutely clean. Sinless, at least for the moment. And all is well with me. I have to do some penance, it stands to reason. But the strange, unforgettable thought alone remains: God so loved the world that he sent his Son into our midst, and at a price of great suffering of his Son reconciled us with himself. Because he did so, JOY springs forth, joy that you barely can catch! That joy is there when you kneel and say, "Lord, I am sorry." The forgiveness of God in his most Holy Trinity covers you.

It is Christ who absolves

Ordination is something mysterious and beautiful. A young man walks up three steps and the bishop puts his hands on his head and the Holy Spirit descends into him. If you have faith, you can see now that Christ enters into that person. You go to the confessional and the priest says "I absolve you," but he isn't absolving: it's Christ who is saying to you that he is absolving you.

The feeling that I have really forgotten God, that I have let him down, saddens us to such a point, or should, that we can't bear it any more. Now what do you or I do? You lay the burden of that tiredness, of that forgetfulness, into the hands of a man who is bound never to talk about it and who represents Christ. The gentle sacrament of Confession, which the Russians call the kiss of Christ, brings you there.

In this part of the world you appraise the priest with your brain. You see a drunken guy staggering at night through a village or your parish; or you know that Father is an alcoholic and not in Alcoholics Anonymous yet. You know a lot of things about the priest. Because you don't approve of who he is, you say to yourself, "Me, go to confession to this guy? Never!" That's because you don't know much about the tenderness of Christ, about what a priest is, about so many things that you should know about.

When the Revolution came to Russia, we were forbidden to go to churches, and forbidden to perform ceremonies. So the Catholic priest would announce that we were going to have a Mass at three or four o'clock in the morning. People would walk in the shadow of the houses and sneak in. Nothing but little tapers were lit by the Blessed Sacrament, and the Mass was very short. One day the door was flung open by Red soldiers just as the priest had consecrated the host and was slowly bringing it down. One shot and the priest was dead, and the Blessed Sacrament rolled on the floor. The Red soldiers walked in, marched to the Blessed Sacrament, squashed it with their heels, turned to us and said, "Where is your God? Under our heels." Then an old man said—I can still hear his reedy voice— "Father, forgive them, even if they know what they do." With that they departed. Little bits of the host were still there. The old man gathered them reverently and gave us Communion. That was the last Communion I had in Petrograd.

We lived under a constant death sentence. Put yourself in that position. If there was only one priest in Petrograd, I would crawl on my belly, even if I knew he had fornicated, committed adultery, was a drunkard, had stolen, had murdered—name the sins—I would crawl on my belly to him. Why? Because he is Christ. He can absolve my sins even while he wallows in his. He can give me the pure Body of Christ, while his hands are dirty. That is the tenderness of Christ to us. That is his love for us. That is why a priest is a priest to us, or should be. I would be idiotic to appraise a priest by the standards of my puny little mind.

When you kneel down and say to a man "I have sinned," you have to believe that he does not exist, that this funny chap—fat, thin, tall, short, whatever he might be—who is called a priest, just isn't there. Sitting there in a chair, is Christ, and it is He who says, "I forgive you." You have to understand what it is all about. It is all about Christ himself. "I absolve you." Get that straight. This must always be there before you in the infinite totality of faith. It isn't the priest who is absolving in confession, it's Christ!

I often listen to the voice of priests who absolve. Some are bored, and some indifferent, and some are happy and rejoice with me. But it doesn't matter, because after all, they don't absolve me, Christ does. But I'm sure that Christ wants them to put a little pep into it, even if they spend two or three or four or fifteen hours in the confessional, like St. John Vianney, the Curé of Ars. He put pep into it, that's how he got canonized. So, a little pep would go a long way.

Remember, Christ chose twelve. One sold him down the river; another denied him. Where were the others when he was arrested? They fled, and you couldn't see them for the dust at their heels. But those are the ones he chose to give us the sacraments.

Forgiveness

I was asking the Lord to help me understand better what the word *forgiveness* means. True, to forgive really is divine. Consider how many times God forgives us. In each of our lives, young or old, we have been forgiven by God one thousand million times, either when we simply said, "I am sorry," or through confession. That is the amazing part about the forgiveness of God. There is just one little thing that we have to do, and that is say two words: "I'm sorry." We commit sin, we say we are sorry, and he forgives us.

Something happens when I say I'm sorry. His forgiveness is like a fire! It goes through me like a fire. But it will not go anywhere, it will be returned, if I do not forgive my neighbor. Christ said, "When you stand in prayer, forgive whatever you have against anybody, so that your Father in heaven may forgive your failings too" (Mark 11:25). Now this is the big challenge of our life. For it is so deeply hidden in hearts that we even think sometimes that it belongs to the psychiatrist, but it doesn't. It belongs to the heart, not to the emotions. If you forgive, perhaps you will never need a psychiatrist. If you forgive your neighbor, you will experience the healing of all the memories which need healing. Forgiveness is something so subtle, so beautiful, so perfect—for when man forgives, he becomes like God.

When the apostles asked Christ how many times they should forgive, he said, "Seventy times seven" (Matt. 18:21–22), which I understand from scripture scholars means "infinitely, without end."

So we are supposed to forgive our brother. We, the unmerciful ones, the proud ones, we are supposed to forgive. The tragedy of many is that they can't forgive, though they know themselves to be forgiven by God. They usually have a scapegoat, and the scapegoat with married people is either the husband or the wife; with priests and religious, it is the superior or bishop. They didn't understand them; they didn't do this, that and the other thing that they should have. They didn't give full recognition, etc.

We have to accept people as they are and start from there, otherwise there is really no forgiveness. It's only lip service, because God accepts me as I am, and he does not compel me to change. He invites me to change.

To forgive is to die to self. To forgive is to grow, grow until we can reach the toes of God! I keep asking people if they believe in God's commandment, "Love your enemies" (Matt. 5:44). If your superior is your enemy, if your wife is impossible, if your husband cannot be trusted, then why don't you begin to believe in what God said? Love your enemies! Perhaps your love will change the face of that "enemy."

The more we forgive, the better we understand God's forgiveness. The more we trust each other, the better we understand God's trust. We should go to the same extent as God—trust the untrustworthy. Simply trust, and then hope will walk with us like a friend, and hope is very musical. It has songs that you have never heard before. It is always a little ahead of you, dancing away with a song so that you can't help but follow it—if you have faith, love, trust, confidence in God.

Now look into your life. I can look into mine. Is there really anything to forgive when you come right down to it? You have to understand something. God uses other people as instruments to make us a little holier. So we owe them a note of thanks! Did you ever consider that?

My father used to say that obstacles are placed before you by God, so that you might overcome them. Anything can become an obstacle. So, he said, just jump over it, don't go around it. Well, he had a good point, he was a wise man. So ever since, I've tried to jump over obstacles. If there is anything to face, I'll say, okay, let's face it. Whenever you have an obstacle, face it directly. Because in the business of Christianity, if the truth is on your side, so is Christ.

Let us truly join hands in deep forgiveness of one another. Let us reconcile ourselves to anyone with whom we are not yet reconciled. Let us forget any attachment to anything that isn't God. Let us enlarge the circle of love in our heart, so that it can encompass humanity, the humanity that flows around, through and by us. Such love is the love of God. Mercy flows from it. Forgiveness is part of it. Humility sings a song to it.

Let us meditate on forgiveness in depth. There is so much to it, because forgiveness comes from Love.

Reconciliation

St. Paul says, "God has reconciled us to himself through Christ, and given us the ministry of reconciliation" (2 Cor. 5:18). This is a fantastic word, my friends. You could almost take it out of context and its sound alone is healing: *reconciliation*. To be reconciled with another. It means forgiving and being forgiven. It means an opening to love on both sides. It really means healing. It is a tremendous word.

We must change our hearts, enlarge them, and allow God to come in, be reconciled with him. What do I mean, be reconciled with him? You know the commandments: love God, love your neighbor as yourself, love your enemies, lay down your life for your brethren. These are the laws of love and these are the ones we have to follow. Unless we follow them we are not reconciled with ourselves, with our neighbor, or with God.

There is a restlessness about us. There are emotional sicknesses that shake us. Because we are not what we should be, the rest of the world is not what it should be, for the fate of the world rests in my sinful hands. If each one of us were what we profess to be—Catholics, Protestants, Jews, or whatever—we would change the world.

We have to come back to reconciliation. Nobody can kiss me unless I want to be kissed. Do we want to be kissed by God? Do we want to be reconciled with him? Do we really want to obey his commandment of love? The word *obey* is silly, because when you love, there is no obedience, in the sense that there is no yoke of obedience. He who loves obeys because he loves.

Will we really be reconciled at Mass? Will we really shed all that junk that fills our minds and hearts and simply say, "Here I am, Lord, such as I am. I am sorry for anything wrong I have done, but I said I was sorry yesterday. I do want to be reconciled with you, because only in accepting the forgiveness of the Father in you will I restore this world to you. There is no other way that I can restore it. As long as I think I can do it on my own, the world will be filled with chaos."

The sacrament of Confession suddenly takes on a tremendous power. It is not just something that one does automatically, or by rote, or because my father or mother taught me. No, the sacrament of Confession is the sacrament of Reconciliation. God comes. God wants to kiss us, embrace us, hold us, like the father when he ran toward the prodigal. But are we ready for the embrace of God? Confession suddenly becomes a cry in the night. There in the quiet night, God descends in Jesus Christ, and suddenly, from all over the world, we walk toward Bethlehem, almost lifted up, crying out in the night: "Here I am. I want to be embraced by you. Hold me tight, so that I never stray away from you." Confession becomes a fantastic gift of God all over again.

Forgiveness of self

Last night I was thinking of reconciliation and wondering what makes reconciliation possible among people. I came to the point that it is forgiveness that makes reconciliation possible. As I prayed a little, it came to me that I have to forgive myself. We have to begin to love ourselves as Christ said, "Love your neighbor as yourself"

(Matt. 22:39). So you must love yourself first.

Take for instance reconciliation. How are you going to be reconciled with your neighbor if you are not reconciled with yourself? What have we got to forgive ourselves for? Well, mostly for the fact that we haven't done the will of God. People who don't do the will of God are the unhappiest, most miserable human beings on earth! Sometimes they know it, and sometimes they don't. Of course, if they don't know it, we have to pray for them, but if they know, then something has to be done to achieve reconciliation. First you have to reconcile yourself with yourself. From thence you can go on to reconciling yourself with the other.

So how about reconciliation with oneself, forgiveness of oneself. Then a new light will rise in us, for our God is a consuming fire, my friends. Let us be consumed with him and we will change the face of the earth.

Reconciliation with others

Next, I have to look around and say "with whom should I be reconciled?" Well, first I should be reconciled with the whole world. And secondly, with the people that are close to me.

For instance, it might be a check-out girl. Say you went to a store and you pushed your cart through and you were impolite to her because she was going in slow-motion. You should go and apologize, and reconcile yourself. There might be a taxi driver that you bawled out. If you can find him again, if he is near your place, go and reconcile yourself. It is not only your friends that you should be reconciled with, but just the ordinary people that pass your way again and again and again.

During Mass we sometimes pray the *Confiteor* so perfunctorily, "I confess to almighty God and to you my brothers and sisters. . ." Suppose we stopped there and really turned to someone. If I feel mad at someone, then I have to get out of my little corner, bow before her and say, "Sorry I was mad at you. Forgive me." It would do us a lot of good if we tried to do that. Christ said, "If your brother has something against you, leave your gifts at the altar, and go and make peace with your brother" (Matt. 5:23–24). One of the reasons why we don't do it is because we are afraid of each other. There is always that horrible fear. Fear of being different. Fear of ridicule. Fear of your age group. There are thousands of fears that come forth and hold us back from God and keep us from opening the door to freedom. Once we get rid of that fear, we are free.

Go to your brother or sister. It might not come off at all. Maybe it will get worse, or people will call you names and throw you out. That happens too. We resent it when people don't come through the way we expect them to. But remember Christ said, "Blessed are you who are persecuted for my name's sake, you will get your reward in heaven" (Matt. 5:11–12). That is what happens when you go to a person to tell him you are sorry, and they throw you out. But you have made it with God. Never mind the person!

You have to reconcile yourself as you walk along the road of life. But even better than reconciliation, is thoughtfulness. You know, I said to myself yesterday, the trouble with us is that we are *thought-less*. Not that we are selfish, not that we are anything like that, we just are without thought! We move, we act, we do things without thought, and we hurt people. We leave misunderstanding. We leave doubt. We leave mistrust. We leave tragedy. That sort of thing cannot happen! We must be *thought-full*, because we are Christians. A Christian is one who is always thinking about the other. God first, my neighbor second, myself last. When we get to that stage, reconciliation is as easy as falling off a log.

Forgiveness comes naturally. In fact, we can't sleep if we don't go and apologize to people, or reconcile ourselves to people. Anything that comes between me and my neighbor divides nations—like a cellophane sheet, we can glare at each other without touching each other. It all begins with me. It is because of me that people are tortured, that people are fleeing their countries. It is because I am not what I should be that all the tragedies of the world happen. Our lack of reconciliation, forgiveness, thoughtfulness, is at the bottom of the world's mess. We haven't got them, and the world is in a mess. And it is, you know!

On us depends the state of the world. Do we, as Christians, as people who believe in God, show the face of Christ on the streets of our cities? Do we? It starts with me, changing my style of life, changing my heart. We need a change of heart even more than a change of lifestyle.

A new creation

"With God every moment is the moment of beginning again." This means that anyone in Christ who is repentant and reconciled is new. Shiny new, like a newly-baptized child. That is one reason why I implore you constantly, and implore God for you constantly, that you get rid of your guilt complexes. How can you have a guilt complex about something that has been confessed, which simply means "opened up," "revealed to God," about something that has been wiped off by him who gives you this shining moment. Every moment is the moment of renewal, if we have forgiveness, repentance, reconciliation. It is so beautiful! It makes you sort of pick yourself up and say, "My God! This is who I am, and this is who my brothers and sisters are." Creation is the making of something from nothing, a new creation. A new creation is the most radical and total type of change that man could conceive. The Lord desires a new order for those coming to new life in his body. His desire for change in our lives far exceeds our own.

Christ is in our midst, and loves us with a tremendous passion. He wants to heal us, change us, make a new creation of us. The Lord desires for us a new heart, committed to him, a realization of being loved and valued by him, and a spirit of loving service to our brothers and sisters.

Freedom

I think of confession as a joyful event. Something glorious. God has forgiven me. Alleluia! Alleluia! Alleluia! It is so exciting. I feel like going to confession again this very minute.

The main thing to remember is that you are talking to God. Saying sorry to anybody is a beautiful thing, but to say "I am sorry" to God is especially beautiful. It makes you free, completely free. Try it sometime. Let that freedom enter your heart and go around saying to yourself, "Alleluia, alleluia, alleluia!"

Books by Catherine Doherty

Madonna House Classics Series:

Poustinia
Sobornost
Strannik
Molchanie
Urodivoi
Bogoroditza

Other Titles:

Dear Father
Dear Parents
Dear Seminarian
Dearly Beloved
Donkey Bells: Advent and Christmas
Doubts, Loneliness, Rejection
Fragments of My Life
The Gospel of a Poor Woman
The Gospel Without Compromise
Grace in Every Season
My Russian Yesterdays
Not Without Parables
Season of Mercy: Lent and Easter
Soul of My Soul
Welcome, Pilgrim

MADONNA HOUSE PUBLICATIONS
COMBERMERE • ONTARIO • CANADA • K0J 1L0

The aim of our publications is to share the Gospel of Jesus Christ with all people from all walks of life.

It is to awaken and deepen in our readers an experience of God's love in the most simple and ordinary facets of everyday life.

It is to make known to our readers how to live the tender, saving life of God in everything they do and for everyone they meet.

Our publications are dedicated to Our Lady of Combermere, the Mother of Jesus and of His Church, and we are under her protection and care.

Madonna House Publications is a non-profit apostolate of Madonna House within the Catholic Church. Donations allow us to send books to people who cannot afford them but most need them all around the world. Thank you for your participation in this apostolate.

To request a catalogue of our current publications, please call (613) 756-3728, or write to us at:

> Madonna House Publications
> 2888 Dafoe Rd
> Combermere ON   K0J 1L0
> Canada

You can also visit us on the Internet at the following address:

> www.madonnahouse.org